Sensing Greatness

Published by Sensing Greatness

© 2022 Patty DeDurr
Illustration © 2022 Eduardo Paj

All rights reserved. No part of this book may be reproduced or transmitted in any form or by any means, electronic or mechanical, including photocopying, recording, or by any information storage and retrieval system, without written permission from the author. For information contact www.sensinggreatness.com

ISBN 978-1-7378622-0-8 (hardcover)
978-1-7378622-2-2 (paperback)

Edited by Katy Nelson
Book Design by Arlene Soto

This Llama Can Write

written by
Patty DeDurr

illustrated by
Eduardo Paj

I have some fun news!

On the last day of the year, there is a tradition on the farm. Each animal writes a letter to thank their favorite farm helper.

The buzz going through the farm is amazing. Everyone is talking about who they want to write letters to and why.

My brain is always so busy thinking about new ideas that it can be hard to focus on just one thing, but today I have an **important job!**

It starts to get really quiet on the farm, and I look around and notice everyone is starting to write already. I hurry to my corner by my best friend **Cria**.

Thank You Letter

{ Date

{ Greeting

{ Who is your helper

Did they solve a problem or fix something?

Why did you choose them?

Questions for your helper

{ Closing

{ Signature

I have a special paper that helps me get all the thoughts out of my head. It has special boxes to help me **organize** my ideas. Cria is having a hard time, so I hand her a special sheet too. Cria says it is **still** too hard.

I give her some different pens to try.
Some are funny looking, some are big,
and some are small.

Cria just sighs and says they
won't help. Writing is still too hard.

We then warm up our hooves to get ready for writing.

We blast off like a rocketship,

hop around like a frog,

 and bounce a ball.

I'm not sure how else to help, but I think and think. That is what is so great about my brain. It is a **great** problem solver.

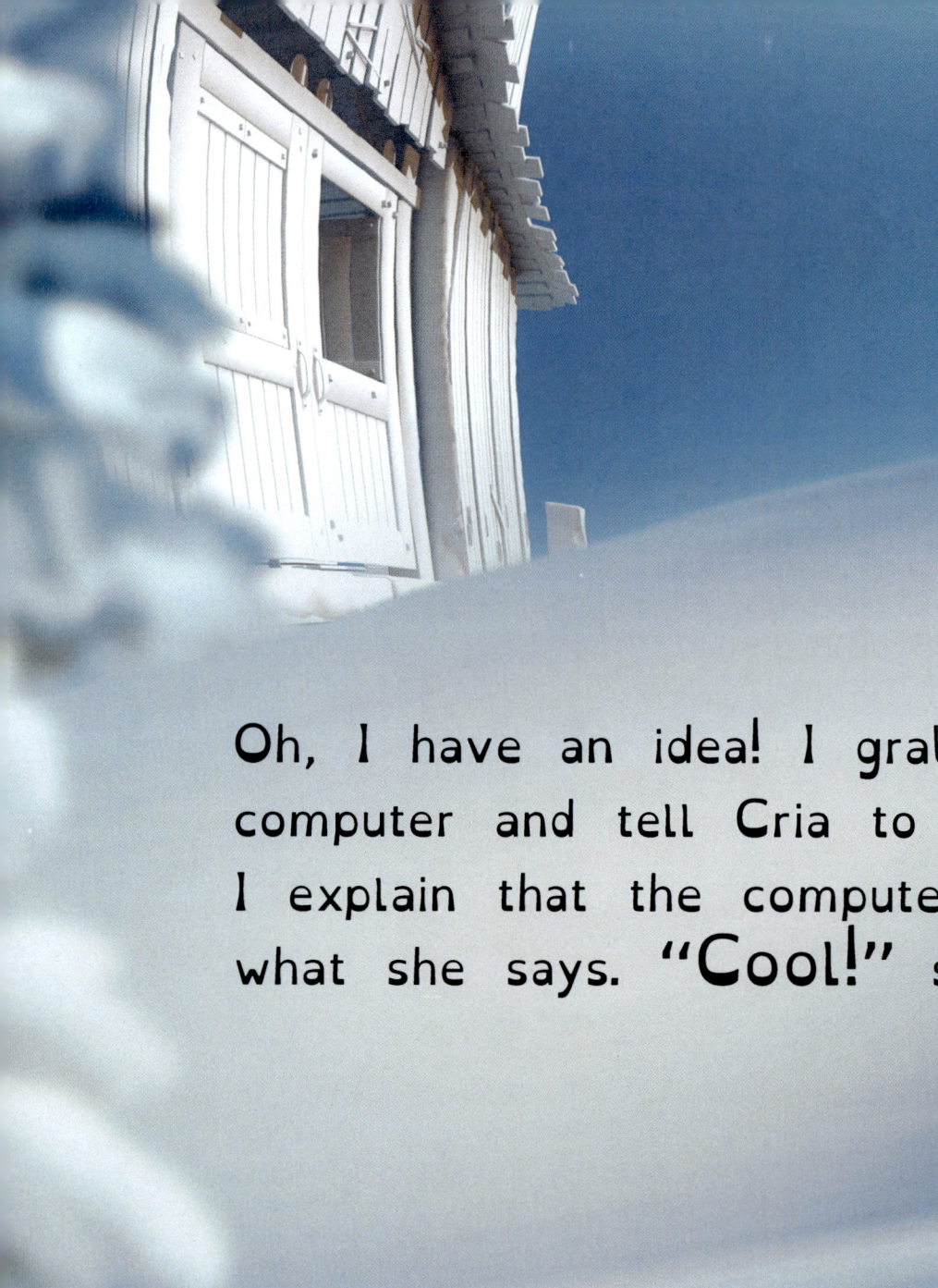

Oh, I have an idea! I grab a computer and tell Cria to talk to it. I explain that the computer will type what she says. "Cool!" says Cria.

After a few minutes, I look over at Cria. She looks upset. She says the computer keeps typing the wrong word when she is speaking. I tell Cria it is okay. We will find a way for her to be a **great** writer.

I open a program that has some fill-in-the-blank sentences to help her brainstorm. It also helps to guess what word she could type. She is **loving** it and says this is so much easier.

After a bit, Cria calls me over.

She is finished with her letter!
I give her a big hug and we celebrate her hard work. Then she shows me the letter, and... it is to me!

Kid,

You are a good friend and my favorite helper on the farm! I think you would make a good teacher. I never liked to write. But, today you were patient with me and used your amazing brain to figure out a solution. I now feel so happy.

I am going to practice writing every day. Will you be my pen pal?

Your friend,
Cria

Who is your helper?

Did you know that in this story, the llama has dysgraphia?

What is Dysgraphia?

- It is a disability that affects your writing ability.
- It can make handwriting challenging, and individuals with dysgraphia may need to use technology to help with writing.
- Some individuals may work with an Occupational/Physical Therapist on fine motor skills and core strength.
- Some individuals may benefit from working on phonological awareness with a Speech Therapist.

Some Dysgraphia Signs

- May hate writing
- Stares at the blank paper
- Letters missing in words
- Some letters are backward when writing
- Does much better when you scribe for them
- Difficulty reading their writing

For a full list of accommodations by grade level, go to
www.sensinggreatness.com

Made in the USA
Las Vegas, NV
23 February 2023